Foundation Stones to Happiness

Essential Principles for a Fulfilling Life

A Modern Translation

Adapted for the Contemporary Reader

James Allen

cooperation. In the characters of the coffee-house, we see a microcosm of global religious dialogue: each voice is confident, each doctrine defended, and yet none are able to reach harmony until they learn to listen. The story becomes a miniature model of what interfaith relations might look like if approached with reverence, curiosity, and humility.

This modern translation has been carefully rendered to preserve the simplicity and clarity of Tolstoy's original narrative while making its language vivid and accessible for contemporary readers. Every effort has been made to retain the spirit of the dialogue and the parabolic force of the closing image, while ensuring that the story's philosophical insight remains intact.

In conclusion, The Coffee-House of Surat is more than a tale—it is a spiritual mirror. It asks each reader to consider: What am I certain of, and why? Do I seek to understand others, or only to defend my position? Can I see truth in the face of someone whose beliefs differ from mine? These are questions that transcend theology and enter the realm of universal ethics. Through this simple coffee-house debate, Tolstoy draws us toward a larger vision: a world where differences in creed are less important than the shared work of compassion, truth-seeking, and love.

priests. But what temple has a basin as vast as the ocean? What roof is greater than the sky? What lamps shine brighter than the sun, moon, and stars? And what images could ever compare to real, living people who love and help one another?

Where can you find clearer proof of God's kindness than the many blessings spread across the world for human happiness? What law is easier to understand than the one written in a person's heart? What sacrifice is greater than the selfless acts of love people do for each other? And what altar is more sacred than the heart of a good person, where God Himself accepts the offering of kindness?

The more a person understands God, the better they will know Him. And the better they know Him, the closer they will come to Him by following His example of kindness, mercy, and love.

So, if someone sees the full light of the sun filling the world, they should not mock or look down on those who only see a small ray of that light in their idols. They should not even despise those who are blind and cannot see the sun at all."

The Chinese scholar, a follower of Confucius, spoke these words. And after that, everyone in the numbers, and the smartest minds still use the same 26 letters. The basics are always simple and few, but without them, there is no knowledge or success. The basic principles in life are also simple, and mastering them is key to building a strong character and lasting success. If you can apply these principles to all areas of life, you will avoid confusion and build a foundation for success.

The first principle is duty. It may be an overused word, but it holds great value for those who follow it with dedication. Duty means taking care of your own responsibilities and not meddling in others' business. The person who's always offering free advice on how others should manage their lives is often the one who struggles with their own. Duty also means focusing fully on what's in front of you, doing your work with thoroughness, accuracy, and efficiency. While everyone's duties may be different, the principle remains the same: knowing and handling your own responsibilities better than anyone else can.

The next principle is honesty. This means being truthful, not cheating or deceiving others in any way. It includes sincerity—saying what you mean and meaning what you say. Honesty rejects flattery and manipulative behavior. It builds a good reputation, and a good

Table of Contents

Table of Contents

Preface - Message to the Reader

Rebuilding the Greatest Library in Human History

Thousands of years ago, the Library of Alexandria was the heart of global knowledge — a sanctuary where the wisdom of every known civilization was gathered and shared freely.

And then, it was lost.

Now, we're rebuilding it — and you are invited to join us.

At the Library of Alexandria, we've set out to make every book available to *every person on Earth* — not just in print, but in every language, every format, and for every reader.

Here's how we do it:

- **Deluxe Print Editions at True Printing Cost** - Order any book as a high-quality paperback, elegant hardcover, or stunning boxset — and only pay what it costs to print. No markups. No middlemen.
- **Unlimited Access to the Greatest Works** - Enjoy thousands of timeless classics — from Plato to Shakespeare to Tolstoy — in beautiful, modern eBook and audiobook editions. Read and listen without limits — for every reader, everywhere.
- **Modern Translations for Every Language & Dialect** - We're reimagining the classics in clear, accessible language — and translating them into every dialect imaginable. Everyone deserves to understand humanity's greatest ideas.

When you visit **LibraryofAlexandria.com**, you're not just accessing books — you're joining a global movement to restore, preserve, and share the wisdom of civilization.

Join us today at LibraryofAlexandria.com

Together, we'll ensure the light of human wisdom never fades again.

With gratitude,
The Modern Library of Alexandria Team

Visit:

www.libraryofalexandria.com

Or scan the code below:

Introduction

Building a Life of Joy from the Inside Out: James Allen's Enduring Blueprint for Fulfillment

James Allen's Foundation Stones to Happiness and Success stands as a brief but powerfully concentrated manual for living with purpose, peace, and personal integrity. Unlike longer philosophical works that explore spiritual development through layers of narrative or abstraction, this book operates like a crystalline guidebook—a focused map pointing directly to the core building blocks of a truly joyful life. Each "stone" in Allen's foundation represents a principle of thought, behavior, and moral orientation that, if firmly set, supports the entire structure of a meaningful, prosperous, and harmonious existence.

Originally published in the early 20th century, Foundation Stones to Happiness was created during a time of social transformation, yet it remains astonishingly relevant to today's world. In the face of modern pressures—constant connectivity, superficial success, emotional exhaustion—Allen's calm and reasoned voice reminds readers that happiness does not come from wealth, entertainment, or prestige. Instead, it emerges from within, through habits of character, moral clarity, and mental self-discipline. He urges us to stop searching outward and begin building inward.

This modern edition, Essential Principles for a Fulfilling Life – A Modern Translation – Adapted for the Contemporary Reader, aims to make Allen's timeless lessons immediately accessible without diluting their depth or strength. His original language is elegant but occasionally archaic; this translation preserves his spiritual rigor while adapting the text into language that today's readers will find clear, direct, and impactful. What remains is the powerful essence of Allen's teachings—a prescription for happiness based on self-mastery, ethical living, and steady inward growth.

The Seven Stones:
Principles That Ground the Joyful Life

Allen structures this book around seven foundational "stones," each representing a virtue or mental state that must be developed and sustained to achieve genuine happiness and success. These are: Right Principles, Sound Methods, True Thought, True Speech, Good Behavior, The Right Occupation, and Purity. Together, they form a comprehensive framework for self-development that balances practical living with spiritual elevation.

Right Principles is the cornerstone, reminding us that all personal growth begins with truth. Without truth, no lasting success can stand. Allen emphasizes that honesty with oneself is the starting point of wisdom—and that all outer achievement must rest on inner integrity. It is through this commitment to truth that we begin the journey of real transformation.

Sound Methods follows, addressing the need for consistency and order in our actions. Allen warns against chaotic living and urges readers to approach life methodically, with intention and focus. Just as an architect needs a blueprint, so too must the individual build a life with structure and clarity.

True Thought and True Speech explore the power of the mind and the spoken word. Allen holds that thoughts shape destiny, and words reveal the heart. Therefore, we must think with precision and speak with integrity, knowing that both habits have the power to either elevate or degrade our inner life.

Good Behavior and The Right Occupation examine how ethical action and purposeful work contribute to fulfillment. Allen argues that no happiness can be sustained without personal virtue and honest labor. Work, when done with care and honor, becomes not a burden but a pathway to spiritual dignity.

Finally, Purity is described as the unifying element that harmonizes all the others. Purity in thought, emotion, intention, and deed brings light to the soul and clarity to the mind. It allows one to experience peace regardless of external conditions and is the clearest signal of one's alignment with the higher self.

Together, these seven stones represent not a checklist but a lifestyle. Allen does not present quick solutions or shallow affirmations. Instead, he offers a path of personal responsibility, moral focus, and inner cultivation—one that leads inevitably to happiness not because of external rewards, but because it is grounded in universal law.

Why These Foundational Teachings Still Matter

In a time when many seek shortcuts to fulfillment or confuse pleasure with happiness, Foundation Stones to Happiness provides a rare and necessary counterpoint. Allen reminds us that the work of becoming happy is internal, continuous, and ethical. There are no secrets or hidden systems. There is only the steady work of aligning thought, speech, and action with the truths that elevate the soul.

The brevity of this work makes it ideal for daily reading and lifelong contemplation. Each chapter can be used as a prompt for personal reflection or spiritual practice. While small in size, the book contains vast reservoirs of wisdom—distilled insights that can quietly reshape a life when applied with sincerity.

This modern edition is designed to keep Allen's timeless message alive for the reader who wants to build a life not on distraction or ambition, but on clarity, virtue, and resilience. It invites us to lay down the stones of our inner structure carefully, deliberately, and joyfully—knowing that a solid foundation will support us through all the changes and challenges life may bring.

Foundation Stones to Happiness deserves its place among the greatest works of spiritual self-development. It is direct without being rigid, humble without being weak, and demanding without being harsh. Allen's voice continues to call us toward the truth: that happiness is not found—it is made. And it is made not by accident, but by building daily with intention, with wisdom, and with love.

Chapter 1
Right Principles

It's important to know what comes first and what to do first. Starting something in the middle or at the end only leads to confusion. Imagine an athlete trying to win by starting at the finish line—it wouldn't work. He has to start at the beginning, and even then, a good start is key to winning. In the same way, a student doesn't start with algebra or literature, but with basic counting and learning the alphabet. Life works the same way—the businessperson who starts at the bottom achieves lasting success, and those who reach the highest levels of spiritual understanding are the ones who have patiently learned the smaller, everyday lessons first. They don't ignore the common experiences that teach them along the way.

The first step to living a good and successful life is to start with the right principles. Without these, bad practices will follow, leading to a confused and unhappy life. Think of it this way: all the math used in business and science comes from the same ten numbers, and all the books that exist are built from the 26 letters of the alphabet. The best astronomers still use the ten reputation leads to success and happiness. Who has truly mastered honesty?

Economy is the third principle. While it begins with managing money wisely, it goes beyond that. It's about preserving your energy—physically and mentally. It's about avoiding harmful habits and wasteful indulgences. By practicing economy, a person gains strength, endurance, and the ability to achieve more. Who has realized the power of economy?

The next principle is liberality. This doesn't conflict with economy, but rather complements it. Only someone who practices economy can truly afford to be generous. A wasteful person has nothing left to give. Generosity is more than just giving money; it's about giving your time, your thoughts, your kindness, and showing goodwill—even to those who oppose you. Generosity builds strong friendships and offers comfort in difficult times. Who has fully grasped the reach of liberality?

The final principle is self-control. This is perhaps the most important of all. A lack of self-control causes untold misery and failure. The businessperson who loses their temper over small issues is already on the path to failure. If everyone practiced even a little self-control, anger and its destructive effects would vanish.

Self-control teaches patience, purity, kindness, and perseverance, and without mastering it, success and stability are uncertain. Who has perfected self-control? Whoever has, is truly a master of life.

These five principles are not just ideas but practices. They are paths to achievement and sources of wisdom. As the saying goes, "Practice makes perfect," and to truly understand these principles and benefit from them, you must not only speak of them—you must live them out in your actions.

Chapter 2
Sound Methods

When the five Right Principles are fully understood and practiced, they lead to Sound Methods. Right principles show themselves in harmonious actions, and method in life is like law in the universe. Everywhere in the universe, parts work together harmoniously, and this order and balance create a cosmos instead of chaos. The same is true in human life. The difference between a true life and a false one, or a purposeful life and a weak one, lies in method. A false life is a confusing mix of thoughts, passions, and actions, while a true life is an orderly arrangement of all its parts. It's like comparing a pile of scrap metal to a well-functioning machine. A perfectly working machine is not only useful but admirable, while one with broken parts is useless and thrown away. In the same way, a life that is organized and efficient is powerful and beautiful, but a life that is confused and inconsistent is just wasted energy.

If you want to live a meaningful life, method must guide every detail of it, just like order governs every detail of the universe we are a part of. One difference between a wise person and a foolish one is that the wise person pays close attention to small details, while the foolish one overlooks them or ignores them entirely. Wisdom comes from keeping things in their proper order and place, no matter how big or small they are. When we break this order, confusion and unhappiness follow.

A good businessperson knows that being organized is a big part of success, and that disorder leads to failure. A wise person knows that living a disciplined, orderly life is key to happiness, while living carelessly leads to misery. A fool is someone who thinks carelessly, acts impulsively, and lives without order. A wise person is someone who thinks carefully, acts calmly, and lives with consistency.

True method doesn't stop with organizing your material things and outside relationships. That's only the beginning. It extends to the mind—organizing your thoughts, controlling your passions, choosing your words carefully, and making good decisions.

To live a sound, successful, and fulfilling life, you must start by paying attention to the little things. For example, what time you wake up and how consistently you do it matters. So do the times you go to bed and how many hours of sleep you get. Regular meals and mindful eating affect your digestion and overall health.

These details may seem small, but they have a big impact on your mental and physical well-being. Structuring your day—whether it's work, rest, solitude, or social time—helps reduce stress and increases productivity, joy, and success.

But this is just the beginning of the method that covers all aspects of life. When this order and logical approach extend to your words, actions, thoughts, and desires, wisdom replaces foolishness, and power comes from what used to be weakness. When a person organizes their mind and creates harmony within themselves, they reach the highest levels of wisdom, efficiency, and happiness.

However, to reach this point, one must start from the beginning. You have to organize and smooth out the small details of life first, then move forward step by step. Each step you take will bring more strength and happiness.

To sum up, method creates the smoothness that leads to strength and efficiency. Discipline is applying method to the mind, which brings calmness, power, and happiness. Method is following a system; discipline is living by rules. But working and living aren't separate— they are two sides of the same thing: character and life.

So, be organized in your work, accurate in your words, and logical in your thinking. The difference between success and failure, harmony and chaos, happiness and misery lies in how methodical and disciplined you are.

Using sound methods in how you work, act, and think—basically, how you live—is the surest way to achieve good health, lasting success, and peace of mind. Building on unsound methods leads to instability, fear, and unrest, even if it seems successful at first. And when failure comes, it hits hard.

Chapter 3
True Actions

When someone strives to understand true principles and work with sound methods, they will soon realize that the details of their actions matter and cannot be ignored. These details can either create something good or lead to destruction, depending on their nature. This understanding of the importance of every action will gradually become clear, giving them new insight and knowledge. As they gain this understanding, their progress in life will be faster, their path more certain, and their days more peaceful. They will act in the right way, unaffected by the external pressures around them. This doesn't mean they won't care about the well-being and happiness of others; rather, they won't be swayed by others' opinions, ignorance, or uncontrolled emotions. True actions are about acting rightly towards others, and those who do what is right know that their actions, based on truth, are ultimately for the good of those around them, even if someone close to them might try to convince them to act otherwise.

True actions can be easily distinguished from false ones by anyone who wants to recognize them in order to avoid the bad and embrace the good. Just as in the material world we choose things by their shape, color, and size, in the spiritual world of deeds, we can identify good and bad actions by their nature, purpose, and effect. We can choose the good and ignore the bad.

In all forms of progress, avoiding the bad comes before accepting and understanding the good, just as a student learns how to do things right by having their mistakes pointed out first. If someone doesn't know what's wrong or how to avoid it, how can they know what's right and how to practice it? Bad or false actions come from focusing only on one's own happiness, disregarding the happiness of others. They arise from strong emotions, unlawful desires, or actions that need to be hidden to avoid negative consequences. Good or true actions, on the other hand, stem from considering others, using calm reasoning and moral principles. They are actions that can be carried out openly, without fear of shame.

A person who acts rightly will avoid actions that bring annoyance, pain, or suffering to others, even if those actions seem small. They will first stop doing selfish and false things, and through this, they will learn to do unselfish and true things. They will learn not to act out of anger, envy, or resentment, but instead will calm their mind before taking action. Most importantly, they will avoid, as they would avoid drinking poison, any actions of trickery, deceit, or dishonesty. These types of actions may seem to bring personal gain but eventually lead to exposure and shame. If someone feels the need to hide what they're doing or knows they couldn't defend it if questioned, they should recognize that it's a wrong action and abandon it immediately.

By following the principle of honesty and sincerity, they will also become more thoughtful about their actions. This will help them avoid getting caught up in the deceptive practices of others. Before signing papers, entering agreements, or making commitments—especially with strangers—they will carefully examine the situation to understand exactly what they are agreeing to. For those who seek to act rightly, carelessness is like a crime. Many actions done with good intentions lead to bad outcomes because they are thoughtless. As the saying goes, "The road to hell is paved with good intentions." The person who acts with true intentions is, above all, thoughtful: "Be as wise as serpents and as harmless as doves."

Thoughtlessness covers a wide range of actions. Only by becoming more thoughtful can a person begin to understand the nature of their actions and gain the ability to consistently do what is right. It's impossible for someone to be thoughtful and still act foolishly. Thoughtfulness and wisdom go hand in hand.

It's not enough for an action to be motivated by good intentions; it must come from careful thought to be a true action. A person who wants lasting happiness for themselves and to do good for others must focus only on true actions. Saying, "I did it with the best of intentions," is a weak excuse for someone who has thoughtlessly gotten involved in the wrongdoing of others. Their hard-earned experience should teach them to be more thoughtful in the future.

True actions come from a true mind. As a person learns to tell the difference between false and true actions, they are also improving and strengthening their mind. This process makes their mind more harmonious and effective. As they gain the ability to clearly see what is right in every situation and the confidence to follow through with it, they are building a strong character and life on a solid foundation. This foundation will not be shaken by failure or persecution.

Chapter 4
True Speech

Truth is understood only through practice. Without sincerity, there is no way to understand truth, and speaking truthfully is the first step toward sincerity. Truth, in its simple and pure form, is about letting go of everything that is false and committing to only what is true. Speaking truthfully is one of the first steps on the path of truth. Lies, deceit, slander, and all forms of harmful speech must be completely abandoned before a person can begin to experience even a small amount of spiritual awakening. A liar and a slanderer are lost in darkness, so deep that they can't tell the difference between good and bad. They even convince themselves that their lies and harmful words are necessary or good because they think they are protecting themselves or others.

Anyone who wants to study "higher things" should first look within and make sure they aren't fooling themselves. If someone speaks words that deceive, or if they talk badly about others—whether from insincerity, jealousy, or malice—then they have not yet begun their spiritual journey. They might be studying things like metaphysics, miracles, or astral travel. They might be learning how to communicate with unseen beings or produce unusual phenomena, or even studying spirituality as a topic from books. But if they lie or gossip, they haven't yet grasped the higher truths. The real higher things are honesty, sincerity, innocence, purity, kindness, gentleness, faithfulness, humility, patience, compassion, sympathy, selflessness, joy, goodwill, and love. To study, know, and live these qualities, one must practice them. There is no other way.

Lying and harmful speech are signs of deep spiritual ignorance, and there can be no spiritual awakening while they are practiced. Their roots lie in selfishness and hatred. Slander is similar to lying but can be even more harmful because it often comes from feelings of anger and can look like truth. It traps many people who wouldn't knowingly tell a lie. There are two sides to slander—there is the person who creates or repeats it, and then there is the person who listens to it and believes it. Slander cannot exist without someone to listen. Harmful words need someone willing to hear them in order to grow, so the person who listens to and believes slander is just as responsible as the one who speaks it. The speaker is an active slanderer, and the listener is a passive one. Together, they spread evil.

Slander is a common and serious problem. It usually begins with misunderstanding. Someone feels wronged, and in anger and resentment, they complain to others, exaggerating the wrong they believe was done to them. Others listen and sympathize, and without hearing the other side, they change their opinion of the person being spoken about. They repeat the story, and with each telling, the details become more distorted, until a completely untrue version of events is being spread.

Slander causes harm because many people, who are not intentionally doing wrong, don't realize the evil they are falling into by allowing themselves to be influenced against someone they once respected. This can only happen among those who have not yet fully embraced the virtue of speaking the truth, which comes from a truth-loving mind. When someone who has not yet freed themselves from believing or repeating slander hears something negative said about them, their mind burns with anger, their sleep is disturbed, and their peace of mind is lost. They believe their suffering is caused by the person who spoke badly about them, but in truth, the root of their suffering lies in their own willingness to believe slander about others.

A virtuous person, someone who has fully embraced truthfulness and refuses to engage in harmful speech, cannot be harmed or disturbed by any negative things said about them. Even if their reputation is temporarily damaged in the eyes of those who are quick to believe the worst, their integrity remains intact, and their character is unspoiled. No one can be harmed by another person's wrong actions—only by their own. So, through all the misrepresentations, misunderstandings, and insults, they remain calm and without revenge. Their sleep is undisturbed, and their mind remains at peace.

Speaking truthfully is the first step toward living a pure, wise, and well-ordered life. Anyone who wants to live a pure life and reduce the suffering in the world must give up lying and slander, even in their thoughts and words. They should avoid anything that even appears to be dishonest or harmful. Half-truths are the most dangerous kinds of lies and slanders. A person should not be a participant in harmful speech by listening to it. They should also have compassion for those who speak harm, knowing that such people are only causing themselves more suffering and unrest. A liar cannot experience the joy of truth, and a slanderer cannot enter the kingdom of peace.

A person's spiritual state is shown by the words they speak, and by those same words, they are ultimately judged. As the great teacher of Christianity said, "By your words, you will be justified, and by your words, you will be condemned."

Chapter 5
Equal-Mindedness

Being calm and steady in all situations means being at peace, because a person can't truly be peaceful if they let their mind get upset or thrown off balance by what happens around them. A wise person stays calm, meets everything with a mind free from bias, and doesn't let emotions control them. They don't take sides or argue to defend themselves; instead, they understand and sympathize with everyone.

A partisan person is so sure that their opinion is right and that anyone who disagrees is wrong, that they can't see any good in other perspectives. They are always in a state of defending or attacking and never experience the quiet peace of having a balanced mind.

The person who keeps a balanced mind watches themselves carefully to avoid letting emotions or biases take over. This helps them develop understanding for others, and as they understand people better, they realize how pointless it is to condemn them. This leads to a feeling of universal kindness that extends to all living beings.

When someone is controlled by strong emotions and biases, they can't see things clearly. They only see the good in their own view and the bad in others. This blindness prevents them from understanding themselves or others, and they feel justified in condemning those who disagree. Over time, this grows into hatred, separating them from others and trapping them in a small, self-made prison of suffering.

The days of a balanced person are sweet and peaceful, full of goodness and blessings. Guided by wisdom, they avoid the paths that lead to hatred, sorrow, and pain. Instead, they follow those that lead to love, peace, and happiness. Life's events don't upset them, and they don't grieve over things that others see as terrible but are just part of life. They aren't overly excited by success or crushed by failure. They see everything in life in its proper place and have no room for selfish desires, regrets, unrealistic hopes, or childish disappointments.

How can this balanced state of mind and life be achieved? It comes only by overcoming one's own weaknesses and purifying the heart. Purifying the heart leads to clear, unbiased understanding, which brings a balanced mind, and that, in turn, leads to peace. A person ruled by emotions is helpless, carried away by passion, while the pure person guides themselves to a safe harbor of calm. The foolish person says, "I have an opinion," but the wise person quietly goes about their work.

Chapter 6
Good Results

Many events in life come to us without us directly choosing them, and we often think they have nothing to do with our choices or character, as if they happen by chance. We call some people "lucky" and others "unlucky," as if they received something they never earned or caused. But when we think more deeply and understand life better, we realize that nothing happens without a cause, and everything is connected by a perfect balance of cause and effect. This means that everything that happens to us is closely tied to our will and character. In fact, the events we don't choose are the results of our own thoughts and actions. This may not seem obvious at first, but many natural laws, even in the physical world, are not immediately clear. Just like we need study and experiments to understand how one physical thing is connected to another, we also need thought and practice to understand how one mental state leads to another. These mental laws are understood by those who practice right actions and have a thoughtful mind.

We harvest what we plant. The things that come to us, even if we didn't directly choose them, are things we caused. For example, a person who becomes an alcoholic didn't choose to have delirium tremens or mental breakdowns, but they caused it through their actions. In this case, the law is obvious to everyone, but even when it's not so obvious, it's still true. Inside ourselves is the root cause of all our suffering and the source of our joy. If we change the way we think, the world around us will stop causing us pain. If we make our hearts pure, everything around us will be pure, and all events will feel happy and in the right order.

Our lives are good or bad, free or trapped, based on the thoughts that cause our actions, because our actions come from our thoughts, and the results of those actions are fair. We can't force good results to happen and take them like a thief. We have to create them by causing the right things inside ourselves.

People try hard to get money, happiness, and wisdom, but they often fail, while others seem to get these blessings without even trying. This happens because the first group has created causes that stop their wishes from coming true. Every life is like a perfectly woven network of causes and effects, efforts (or lack of efforts) and results. Good results can only come from starting good efforts and causes. A person who lives by right actions and follows sound methods based on correct principles won't need to fight or struggle for good results. They will come naturally as the result of a righteous way of living. They will harvest the rewards of their actions with joy and peace.

This idea of sowing and reaping, even in the moral sense, is simple, but many people are slow to understand and accept it. We've been told that "the children of darkness are wiser in their day than the children of light," meaning that people often follow the law of cause and effect in material matters but ignore it in spiritual ones. For example, no farmer would expect to harvest where they didn't plant, or to plant weeds and harvest wheat. Yet, in their spiritual lives, people do wrong and expect good things to come from it, and when the bitter results come, they complain about how unfair life is. They often blame others for their suffering, refusing to see that the real cause lies within themselves, in their own thoughts and actions.

Those who are searching for the right way to live and want to become wise and happy must train themselves to follow this law of cause and effect in their thoughts, words, and deeds, just like a gardener follows the law of planting and harvesting. A gardener doesn't question the law; they just follow it. When people start to follow this same law in their minds and actions, it will lead to a harvest of happiness and well-being for all. Just like people obey the laws of nature, we should obey the laws of spirit, because both laws are really the same—they're just different sides of the same principle working in opposite directions.

If we follow the right principles, wrong results can't happen. If we use sound methods, no weak or faulty part can get into our lives, and no bad thing can get into the building of our character to make it unstable. If we do true actions, only good results can come. Saying that good causes can bring bad results is like saying you can plant corn and harvest nettles.

A person who follows these moral principles will gain such insight and balance in life that they will always be happy and peaceful. All their efforts will be well-timed, and the results of their life will be good. Even though they may not become wealthy—nor will they have the desire to—they will find the gift of peace, and true success will come to them as a faithful companion.

Thank you for Reading

You've Just Read a Piece of the Greatest Library Ever Rebuilt

Thank you for reading.

This book is one of thousands we're restoring, reimagining, and translating as part of the **Modern Library of Alexandria** — a global movement to preserve and share humanity's most important ideas.

What was once lost to fire and time is now rising again — not just as memory, but as living, breathing knowledge, freely accessible to all.

What You Can Do Next:

- **Keep Reading.**

  Discover more legendary works — in beautiful print, audiobook, or digital form — at LibraryofAlexandria.com.

- **Build Your Own Library.**

  Every title is available as a paperback, hardcover, or collectible boxset — at true printing cost. Craft a personal library worthy of display.

- **Spread the Light.**

  Share this book. Tell others about the movement. Help us translate every timeless work into every language, so no reader is ever left behind.

By finishing this book, you've already taken part in something extraordinary.

Join us at LibraryofAlexandria.com

Together, we're rebuilding the greatest library the world has ever known.

With appreciation,
The Modern Library of Alexandria Team

Visit:

www.libraryofalexandria.com

Or scan the code below: